Crystal & Sound

Enjoy the subtle effects of rock crystals combined with crystal singing bowls

DICK DE RUITER
TOSCA TETTEROO

Binkey Kok Publications – Havelte/Holland

Text Dick de Ruiter, Tosca Tetteroo
Editing Valerie Cooper
Photography Eelco Boeijinga
Layout and cover design Jaap Koning
Printed and bound in the Netherlands

Published by Binkey Kok Publications – Havelte/Holland
www.binkeykok.com
e-mail info@binkeykok.com
ISBN 90-74597-70-X

CONTENTS

INTRODUCTION

Most people are familiar, one way or another, with rock crystal (quartz), if only in its polished form as decoration or jewelry.

Since ancient times, the sparkling clarity of this stone has had a very special allure to people all over the world. Nowadays, even though things are changing at an impossible pace, the age-old crystal still appeals to us because of its outer beauty and its great energetic powers. If we open up ourselves to this, beautiful things can happen. This is what this booklet is about; and you can experience those beautiful things yourself by listening to the accompanying CD of crystal singing bowls. In chapter 7, you will find some ways to use the CD and crystal power. Much is possible if you use the power of rock crystal wisely.

In my work as a gem therapist and crystal healer,[1] I have utilized this power for many years. By tuning in to it, I have developed various healing methods. Even now I am amazed, again and again, when I work with these special powers. Most of all it is the purity of rock crystal that touches me deep inside; the age-old beauty, grown in the depths of our earth, containing so much light power, so much concentrated information.

A rock crystal makes me humble, and I feel thankful when I get the chance to be connected with one of them. In mutual respect.

Now there are new instruments, crystal singing bowls, born out of cooperation between our knowledge and the eternity of nature. This will open up new possibilities, new chances.

This booklet does not pretend to be complete; this would be impossible within the limits of its size. Its only aim is to inspire and invite you to experience yourself the clear and sonorous world of rock crystal, which you can hear in its pure form, as well as in its sounding shape: the crystal singing bowl.

The Krater Gem Center, November 2003
– Tosca Tetteroo

---

[1] *Crystal healer:* This term is used throughout this booklet, to describe a therapist who works with crystals, and/or crystal singing bowls.

1 – ROCK CRYSTAL

Rock crystal. Solidified sunlight. See how the sunlight plays with its shafts, how it displays a rainbow of colors. Fabulous! In my workroom this rock crystal pendant is hanging at my windowpane. The opposite wall displays a colorful spectacle, never the same. A wonderful show, just like the rainbow itself. Glancing through the pages of this book also brings joy.

But actually working with rock crystal, directly and through the sound of singing bowls, can also perform miracles. In Ireland and Scotland they are called *"godstones,"* used as a gift to honor the dead at burial sites.

Most rock crystal belongs to the quartz group. Sometimes it is transparent, sometimes only translucent. Some parts of a piece of rock crystal can be clear, while other parts of it have small hazes, or white, growing layers.

Rock crystals have been found all over the world, but the main resource-rich areas are Brazil, Madagascar, and the United States. In former days a lot of it was found in the Swiss alps, including a dark-colored variety, called *morion.* In Carrara, Italy, very small, pure rock crystals known as the "tears of Carrara" are found in its famous marble. Rock crystal can also be found in most plaster (India) and limestone (US, New York), except for in primeval formations. In Brazil, very special rock crystals called "ghost-quartz" have been discovered. These actually come from a crystallization process within an existing larger crystal. Several small crystals float in a cavity of the stone which is filled with fluid or sometimes with gas. Since the invention of artificial crystal quartz in the Bohemian glass industry, the processing of rock crystal has largely come to an end in Europe.

Each crystal has its own "personality" and its own story. Precious stone experts are usually able to see where they come from, which powers they have, and how they can be used.

In its natural, raw form, rock crystal has a six-sided (*hexagonal*) prism shape, coming to a six-sided pyramidal point. These six sides are not always the same size. The number six is frequently found in nature, for instance in the number of tulip, snowdrops, and lily petals, as well as in the points of a snowflake and the cones of the beehive. The number six is called the number of the human on earth: *the incarnated human being*. The hexagon and the six-pointed star—in fact two intertwined triangles—are symbols for the human being in harmony. It has been said that living in six-sided buildings would guarantee a peaceful society. Who would volunteer to experiment with that?! In such a society, crystals would be used as well. . .

Each shape of the pyramid point at one or both ends of a piece of rock crystal has its own meaning and is used for a designated purpose during crystal healings. Worldwide, rock crystal was and is utilized as part of natural healing practices because of its pure, powerful energetic effects.

We are all familiar with the "crystal ball." A clairvoyant will sometimes use a crystal ball as an aid, a portal, to help perceive the information he or she seeks. This is described in chapter 4.

Lenses made of polished rock crystal give the best and purest effects. In electronics the use of crystals has expanded tremendously in the last few decades, because of its ability to store information. Every radio or television, every mobile phone contains a crystal element. It is exactly this ability to store and pass on information that we can use in crystal healing.

In her book, *Practical Use of Singing Bowls*[2] the author Anneke Huyser mentions a special kind of rock crystal, the *Herkimer diamond*, which can create an electromagnetic field in order to transform sound vibrations into healing energy. She writes that rock crystal can have an effect on all energy centers in our body. And singing bowls sound different, more harmonious, when some pieces of rock crystal or tourmaline are placed around it. The stones neutralize the vibrations, and the sound of the bowls becomes more agreeable to our ears.

Even now, the Free Catholic Church still uses different kinds of precious stones, including rock crystal (or diamonds), at the altar and in the bishop's scepter. Astrology links rock crystal to the sign Gemini, and sometimes also to the sign Leo. •

---

[2]See the Reading List in the back of this book.

2 – THE HEALING EFFECTS OF ROCK CRYSTAL

The expression "healing effects" can be taken literally. Another term used in the alternative health field is "holistic." The whole human being, not just a small part, is involved in the process, made whole, and healed. One whole be-ing.

In the hands of an experienced healer, the radiating, clear rock crystal is an important and effective natural instrument of healing, to be used to realign one's balance. This can be done by applying the pure rock crystal with one hexagonal point, or in special cases hexagonal points at both ends, during healings, or using two specially polished spherical or rounded-off rock crystals. Balls of pure rock crystal are also being used because of their purifying and healing powers.

The healing effect of rock crystal is considerable, and there are many uses and methods for applying them. It can help us become better balanced and experience more mental and physical energy, as well as give our living or working areas a positive energy charge.

Energy often is such a vague concept. Modern Westerners have a tendency to deny the validity of stories about the power of crystals. Our electrical and communication networks, or the power behind a volcano eruption are visible, audible, or sensible, perceptible forms of energy. The term "energy" is likely to become less comprehensible when we think about our already immense, worldwide network of mobile phones—how does it work? We can hardly understand how.

Likewise, the energy in our bodies is hard to describe. Still, it is clear to anyone that without this same energy, life would be impossible. This life energy arises out of our earth, but comes down from the sun as well. We get our energy from our food, which again has been cultivated out of earth energy and sun energy, and from the oxygen we breathe, the same oxygen that has been produced by our vegetable kingdom. Eventually, as we are taught by science, everything can be expressed in terms of energy, and all matter in terms of vibration—harmonic as well as, regrettably, disharmonic vibrations. Who knows what this gigantic mobile phones network eventually can bring about?

This is the way we should also look at rock crystal, as a structure in which light energy, and other sorts of energy as well, flow easily and harmonically in order to be passed on amplified. Included in that energy is the enormous light force the crystal has been able to collect during hundreds of thousands of years.

For ages rock crystal has been used in the optical instruments industry for the making of prisms and lenses. So rock crystal appears to be able to store and pass on a lot of energy. Hence the use of crystal in modern electronics: radio, television, transmitters, mobile phones—all of these contain crystals in one way or another. The crystal healer calls this energy "light energy."

The ability to transmit positive light power is so important in this day and age. But negative energy can also be stored. That is why it is so important to rinse the crystals after a healing session under running water and, if possible, place them in full sunlight for a while.

According to the crystal healers, rock crystal channels and transfers pure sun power. Numerous stories have been recorded, most of them relating to healing diseases and complaints of organs which are energetically connected to the sun: the back, eyes, heart, and solar plexus. Some of these disorders are: dizziness, angina pectoris, restless heart / heart palpitations, cramps, back trouble (mostly vertebral discs), menstrual pains, eczema, elimination of waste products, nervous system complaints, carsickness, fatigue, and depression. Disturbances in the indoor electromagnetic field have been reported to be eliminated by placing large quantities of rock crystal at the points of disturbance.

Rock crystal has a very strong radiance, is perceptible by most people during a healing session. The crystal will, so to speak, harmoniously rearrange the personal vibration and create a new energy flow in areas that had been blocked before. This way, the network of energy flow in the person can be harmonized once more, as it was supposed to be. Only then can true healing occur. Rock crystal can be a handle, an aid in this process.

The crystal healer puts it this way: rock crystal harmonizes and gives lots of new energy to spirit, mind and body. Rock crystal makes WHOLE. And this has nothing, nothing at all, to do with "belief in" or any rituals. This is a pure, experiential happening. That is why there is a CD together with this book: experience it yourself! •

3 – CRYSTAL SINGING BOWLS

The voice of the crystal

In addition to using the natural forms of rock crystal for its good qualities, we can hear and experience the powers of nature in the *sound of crystals*, the voice of the crystal. And this is how it's done:

Crystal singing bowls are made up of almost 100% pure quartz (silicon). Quartz is a coalescence of sand (crystals) and water. The quartz is heated up to about 7232 degrees Fahrenheit, and cast in special molds. The bowls are then tuned to a certain pitch. Using the latest tuning equipment, this can be done meticulously, up to one hundredth of a key—an extremely exacting job, but the results are magically beautiful. Of course these bowls are very vulnerable. The bowls usually are a lovely pure white, and are available in whole sets of all the notes of the musical scale. Usually they are sold in sets of seven, in the pitches of the chakra tones (see further on in this chapter). During last few years, jewel-like bowls have been created in the United States; in addition to the classic white crystal bowls, you can find clear, transparent ones, colored ones (in all colors of the chakras), a fusing of crystal with pure 24K gold (!), or with an alloy of platinum and silver.

The sound experience of these special instruments touches listeners in the depths of their souls. This may sometimes happen with some resistance, as experienced healers know. Some people don't like the sound of crystal singing bowls at all. For them, crystal bowl healing is too confrontational. By handling this very subtly and softly, crystal bowl healers can break such people's resistance within one or two sessions and their appreciation of the sound will change, too. Most people experience the sounds as futuristic, different from any other sound they have heard. In any case, the effects they produce are different from those of any other sound.

Our bodies consist of a large amount of water, over 80%. Everyone knows that when you throw a stone in a pond, the water will ripple. Water vibrates very easily. Just as the tuning fork on a table has the whole tabletop as its sound board, the harmonic vibrations of singing bowls can harmonically resonate the fluids in our body, our bloodstream, and our organs. The larger singing bowls can even vibrate the matter of our bone structure. The vibrations that crystal singing bowls produce are able to get *anything* into harmonic vibration, and let the energy return to its natural flow. Through sound, a new personal vibration can evolve; a vibration that is harmonious and balanced, active and healthy.

The sounds of crystal bowls are very different from those of the Tibetan singing bowls. The first track of the CD provides a clear comparative example. But the effects are different as well.

The sound healer says: "The difference is that Tibetan singing bowls touch and open up your ancient wisdom, your core knowledge. The singing bowls made of crystal will touch you in your be-ing in the present. More in the *here and now*. They will open up to the future."

Energy Centers

From Eastern science we know about the *chakras*, energy centers along the spine, through which energy is absorbed into different areas of our body. For instance, the third chakra in the stomach area will distribute energy to our metabolic system. The energy flow of a certain chakra—and thus also in the related body area—can be influenced positively by a certain tone that resonates with this center. These vibrations are literally perceptible in that body part.

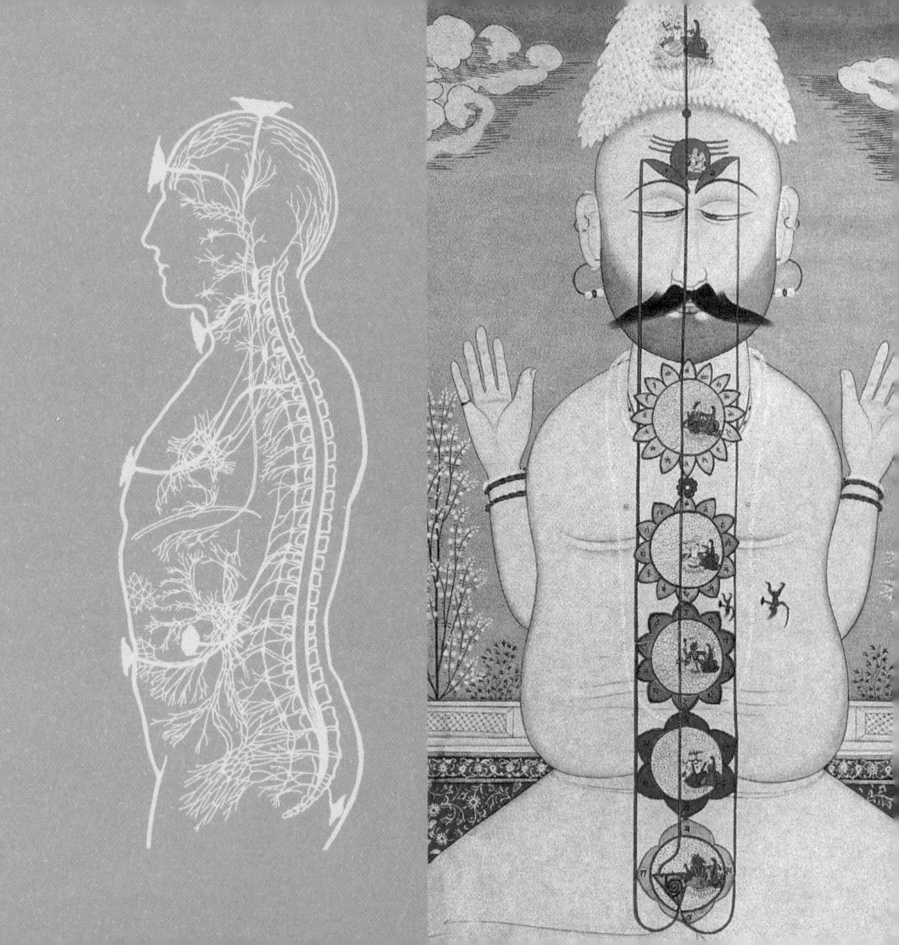

The tones and accompanying colors (light therapy or visualization) are:

1st chakra (around the coccyx): C – red
2nd chakra (around the first vertebrae): D – orange
3rd chakra (stomach area): E – golden yellow
4th chakra (heart area): F – green
5th chakra (neck/shoulders): G – clear blue
6th chakra (eyebrow area): A – violet/pink
7th chakra (top of the head): B – clear white

You can read more about this, and experience the chakra tone effects with the CD *Chakra Delight*, another Book/CD (see Reading List in the back of this book). •

4 – THE CRYSTAL BALL

The word "crystal" is from the Greek *krustallos*, meaning clear ice. Crystal balls are still being made and used. Legends tell us that a crystal ball should be at least two inches in diameter, and be placed on a base of ivory or ebony- or boxwood. It should be completely transparent, spotlessly clear; so clear that the beholder would not be able to tell if it is standing still or spinning. It should be made from pure, carefully extracted (not with explosives) rock crystal. Clairvoyants use crystal balls to gaze into them in order to get clear images of things yet to happen.

As a matter of fact, crystal is not the only medium that is used for gazing into. Hindus gaze into inkblots or syrup; the Romans, Arabs and the English druids studied fingernails, polished stones, soap bubbles, glasses of water or wine. In Greece, people went to see a medium who gazed into a sacred water-well. Still, the real rock crystal ball seems to work best. While the fortune-teller—in the early days these were always women—bends over her ball, she moves her hands around it in order to "charge" it. In the silence that follows, clouds will form inside the ball, enabling the prophetess to receive her images or visions.

It's estimated that about one in twenty people will be able to perceive something in the ball. The crystal ball can be seen as an amplifier of the clairvoyant's ability (*cryptesthesia*), in the same way binoculars help us see things that are far way. It is an object of concentration, in which images will show themselves.

The room in which the ball is used has to be properly prepared. When consulting the crystal ball, never hold it directly in front of the light. The light should be just enough to be able to read. There should not be more than three people in the room—reading for one is more appropriate. The visions that are seen do not seem to follow any law of nature, so one can never foretell which way they will present themselves. It is a mixture of images, feelings, and impressions. The main object is that the crystal gazer is able to concentrate better, so she can perceive the images that come up in a better and clearer way. It cannot be denied that there have been numerous stories of extremely accurate observations and predictions. It remains to be seen whether fortunetellers who use crystal balls really are able to see the future within them. •

5 – SINGING BOWLS CD: CONTENTS AND LISTENING ADVICE

The CD in the back of this book contains three long tracks. Rainer Tillmann is the musician playing the singing bowls. This chapter is about the CD's contents and the instruments, and contains some listening tips.

Rainer Tillmann is a gifted singing bowls player with many years of experience. He discovered singing bowls in the 1980s, when he was playing in a rock band. Since then he has become specialized as a "meditation musician." He discovered the crystal singing bowls in the 1990s, when a process was finally found to make them perfect and finely tuned to a certain pitch. From then on, he has been using these special sound instruments sparingly in his concerts and recordings, alone or in combination with the metal singing bowls, of which he has more than 100 in his collection. There are not many singing bowls players. In Europe and the United States there are no more than 50, of whom the really talented are less than 10. Tillmann stands at the top as a master player.

Singing bowls are usually played in two ways: by striking with (mostly) felt hammers of different sizes and rubbing them with a "gliding stick." The gliding stick is usually a handy piece of spar with a cloth band or suede wrapped around it. Sometimes a violin bow is used.

By striking a bowl we get the effects of a gong. Depending on the size of the bowl, the tones range from subtle, light ones with the little bowls to impressively heavy tones that are literally perceptible in the whole body.

One rubbing technique is similar to the way crystal drinking glasses can be resonated by running a wet finger around the rim, making a tone so intense that the glass sometimes cracks. Rubbing a singing bowl can also be done very lightly and delicately, releasing one basic tone, together with the less audible harmonics, or overtones. Overtones are present in every natural musical instrument, and they will always form a steady pattern. With singing bowls they are easily discernable, and from the purity of these overtone patterns we can hear if it is a good singing bowl or not. It should be perfectly round and u-shaped and the metal ones should be made from one piece of metal.[3]

Another way of rubbing the bowl is done by turning the stick almost vertically along the outside edge of the bowl. With this technique, not only the

---

[3] You can learn more about harmonics in the book/CD *Harmonic Overtone* (see the Reading List in the back of this book).

basic tone but also the overtones—and even the undertones—become quite audible, enough to drown out the basic tone. It takes many years of practice to make this happen correctly and consistently! It goes without saying that the singing bowls themselves need to be of impeccable quality, otherwise the overtones do not match the primary tone and are not very nice to listen to. Pure singing bowls are very difficult to find these days. Newly made (metal) bowls almost never have those pure overtones and resonance as the authentic ones from ages past.

If you plan to buy a singing bowl with which to experiment, please let someone experienced with them advise you. This applies as well to the crystal singing bowls—a crystal bowl should suit you well. Really good singing bowls are not cheap, but compared to the cheaper new ones they are worth the price.

Crystal singing bowls have been made in our time, manufactured with our technology from pure quartz, while the metal singing bowls have been made for ages in Tibet. The crystal singing bowls have a completely different sound and different therapeutic effects. Tibetan singing bowls have a transparent metal sound with very clear overtones, while crystal bowls sound softer, with an unexpected, somewhat milder, full resonance. Although to the untrained ear it sometimes seems as if two or three singing bowls do not match melodically, the harmonic overtones they produce do match perfectly (if carefully selected in the performance, of course!). We are just not used to these harmonic overtones in our Western music, but these bowls resonate in such an intriguing way that even the untrained ear will adapt to them quickly and be able to enjoy them.

How to Listen to the CD

Of course you can just listen to these sound meditations, but they are meant to do much more. They are created for you to experience the harmonizing impact of crystal sound, physically as well as mentally.

The room in which you listen should be pleasantly warm, lights dimmed. The air in the room should be clean; you might want to purify it beforehand with good incense. Your clothes should be comfortable and loose. Make sure you cannot be disturbed. It is best not to eat a lot just before listening.

You can lie down, relaxed on a bed or on a mattress on the floor, so you will not be bothered by tension in your back or shoulders. Lie down with a good support for your back and head. Lying down is associated with going to sleep, so if you wish to experience a sound meditation consciously, it is actually better to listen while sitting upright, so that your breathing will be free, with a good support for your back and buttocks. It is absolutely necessary to be able to listen as relaxed as possible, without any restraint in any part of your body.

The best position is in front of the speakers—one to the right and one to the left. Another possibility is between the two speakers. The ideal situation, of course, is within a good *surround* system!

Good audio equipment is crucial for the physical effects. That is why you need to listen through speaker boxes (20 watts minimum, 50 watts or more is best!) and not through headphones. This way the vibrations are literally sensible, perceptible, in your body. Yet, the volume does not have to be that high. In some cases the sound therapist will find it necessary to play a deep sound at high volume for just a little while, in order to break through an energy block, but usually the volume should be at a level that is still pleasant for the ears. However, too low a volume is not good either, because then the resonance effect (*re-sonare*, "sounding with") will not be achieved.

Always begin the listening session with a little relaxation, a few deep, quiet breaths, particularly breathing out—letting go, possibly a few shoulder and head rolls, and then directing your attention within. Let your breathing continue by itself, as it is being handled from inside. If you feel the urge to now and then take a deep breath and sigh out completely, that is OK too, do not hold back! Open up for the experience you are about to receive.

You can also use the CD to create a harmonious background during a yoga session or a massage. The sound atmosphere seamlessly fits in with the experience of breath and relaxation—delicious!

Although little can go wrong, people who are emotionally or physically unstable should always listen to these sounds with a professional therapist. The sounds can accomplish small miracles, but even miracles sometimes need to be assisted if you want them to happen nicely. And we have experienced miracles with the singing bowls' sounds in institutes for the mentally handicapped and psychiatric patients!

Audio Meditations

The three audio meditations on this CD have been selected for you to experience what crystal sound can do, with or without rock crystals. Between the tracks there is a pause of silence (45 seconds). This has been done intentionally so you can even experience the beautiful silence after the sound—the silence all around, the silence within. After the sound experience, the silence will be even more intense, more perceptible. You might even stop the CD player for a while to keep on meditating in silence.

On the first track, **Into Light & Harmony**, you will hear a curious ensemble of modern crystal singing bowls and the antique metal ones. You will be able to hear the differences between both kinds.

Here, you can imagine the powerful, but quiet, steady growth of our plant kingdom. Out of the dark depths of Mother Earth they grow, reaching out to the light of the sun. In this recording you can feel the plant's longing for the light, for the harmony of the eventual flower. The majestic sounds create an atmosphere of meditative rest and harmony.

This track can be used as a short but powerful meditation of about 10 minutes. It is especially useful, for instance, if you are feeling stuck in certain patterns and would like to grow further, move on, and take the next step in your development.

The second track, **Crystal Lakes**, reflects the water element. It is the longest track of the CD (over 20 minutes), and can be used, for example, with a morning meditation. The harmonic overtones are perfectly balanced so they create a physical and mental harmony, but in an unusual, dreamy atmosphere. It's also very suitable for easing pain, including headaches. Do not try to analyze the sound—just experience it! This piece can also be used as a background or meditative tool along with all kinds of healing practices, or just to relax with.

Track three is **Magic Tree**. The purity of sound is magical, the sounds drifting left to right and back again, up and down. Here the crystal singing bowls are breathing an aura of rest and contemplation. The bowls are subtly being struck and rubbed, while cymbals tinkle like stars in the sky. With these sounds, your mind can be nourished by the earth energy of the trees. Here, your soul can come to rest. This meditation is appropriate for people who wish to get more in touch with their bodies. This is called "grounding." The effects are profound, so this track is meant to be listened to with full attention, being there to feel and experience the sounds. Only in this way will the effects be to full advantage. At the end, you will hear a series of very special harmonic overtones. This sound meditation is 13:25 minutes long.

Total playing time, including silence in between tracks: 46:04 minutes. •

6 – HEALING WITH ROCK CRYSTAL AND CRYSTAL SINGING BOWLS

What follows is a description of the many possible procedures a therapist might use while working with rock crystal and crystal singing bowls. As this is the therapist's specialty, he or she knows exactly what to do, the order and positioning, the sound combinations, intensity, and duration of the treatment. Such a treatment should be administered only by a professional. Other methods that anyone can use are described in chapter 7.

During treatment, the therapist places the singing bowls around the person, who is either sitting or lying down. With the person lying down, the therapist can place the crystals on crucial places on the body. The therapist will choose these crystals intentionally, in order to supply or drain energy, or give an intensive impulse for just a short while in order to break through an energy block. Then the singing bowls will be struck or rubbed in a particular order. Sometimes the therapist will take a bowl in his or her hand and hold it close to a certain body part, so the sound vibration can penetrate deeply into the tissues involved, and can literally be sensed by the client. A strongly vibrating singing bowl can also be moved slowly along the body, either upward or downward.

During healings with rock crystals, the therapist will use a singing bowl that is connected with the chakra that is out of balance. The therapist might strike the bowl with a special mallet or a specially made stick wrapped in suede. The difference lies in the intensity of the sound. The strike is short and very powerful. The reverberation with the overtones of such a strike can continue for three or four minutes. The rubbing technique with the stick gives a softer but penetrating and long lasting sound. The vibrations will massage the body in a pleasant, harmonic way. So we can literally call this a *sound massage.*

Some people might initially experience the sound as unpleasant. Only when a renewed energy flow has been established by the sounds and the crystals, and certain blockages have been removed, will the sound be agreeable again, pleasant to hear and feel.

During such a treatment, which on average takes about half an hour, much can be released. Blocks are being cleared away, creating a healthy, balanced flow in all chakras. Then there will be room for growth and regeneration. •

7 – METHODS FOR SELF-HEALING WITH CRYSTAL SINGING BOWLS

You can experiment with experiencing what crystals can do for you. Of course, your possibilities may be limited: good crystals are costly and good crystal singing bowls are outright expensive. Still, it is possible. Even if you already own some crystals and/or bowls, you should seek the guidance of an experienced crystal healer to determine how you should use and place the rock crystals. Afterwards, you may apply the crystals yourself of course, on your-

self, your friends, or loved ones.

You can work with the crystal sounds by using one or more tracks of the accompanying CD. You will find a description of the tracks in chapter 5, with advice on which sound equipment you should use.

A very simple but good method is sitting or lying down, in front of or in between the speakers, and directing your attention completely to your breathing. Tracks 1 and 3 are most suitable for such a session. Set the volume at a pleasant level. Now try to breathe consciously, but completely relaxed. Let the breath flow deeply into your chest and then all the way to your belly. Imagine that with your inhalation, new, recharging energy flows into your body. With each exhalation, the tensions flow out of your body into the Earth beneath you. Meanwhile, part of your attention will experience the vibrations of the singing bowls. Try to locate where a sound is resonating in your body—it could be either very vague or very localized. If you feel tension somewhere, direct your energy to that area for a while and release the tension with your next exhale. Beginners can breathe deeply like this for about ten to twenty rounds, while experienced breathers can continue to about fifty deep breaths. Then, as long as the sounds continue, let your breath regain its natural rhythm. Be aware and observe.

This session can work well in cases of chronic fatigue or burnout, when the body is exhausted and there is no energy flow. The mind is tense and the soul craves help. All the chakras are out of balance and have too little energy left to cooperate correctly. In such a case, it is a blessing to recharge regularly with rock crystal and the crystal singing bowls.

When you are the lucky owner of a favorite singing bowl, you can best use it while sitting down. Place the bowl on a platform, table, or stool, at the body height you desire. After some preparation such as relaxing, calm and deep breathing, and emptying the mind, you can now strike or rub the bowl. Always let the sound completely resonate until it is gone. The more intensive the touch or sound, the more powerful the energy flow will be. In order to receive the bowl's calming effects, you need to play it softly. You will learn by experience what you need and which procedure or approach will work best for you. •

8 – MEDITATION

Inspiration from Tosca Tetteroo

Listening to a range of singing bowls that cover all the tones of the musical scale is a very special and deep experience—enchanting and touching at the same time.

Meditation is really nothing more than directing your attention inward in a relaxed way. You can do it while lying down, but it's best to sit up straight. Listen to the sounds of the crystal singing bowls. Feel what is happening with you while listening and experiencing the tones. Try not to think at all, and enjoy deep draughts of what you hear and feel.

Listening regularly to the song of the crystal gives you inspiration, rest, vigor, and harmony—a whole, delicious feeling of being here and now. As a meditation, listening to the crystal singing bowls is very clarifying. You will sort of float along with the sounds resonating through your body, you will listen to your own self, your deepest self. Here and now. To be here and now, being in the body and experiencing this, that is the power of the crystal. Crystal clear!

In order to go through the meditation even more intensely, you can also include the natural one-pointed rock crystals. By doing so, you will generate a strong energy flow that is very perceptible and lasting. This is a particularly good method during periods when you need extra energy.

Energy Flow with Two Single-pointed Rock Crystals

For this meditation you need two similarly-sized, regularly shaped single-pointed crystals. Choose a size that fits comfortably in your hands.

- Sit or lie down and relax. Make sure that the room is warm enough, that you will not be disturbed for a while, the lights are dimmed, and if needed, wrap a blanket around you. Select a track from the CD (track 2 is very appropriate) and set your player at a pleasant volume.
- Breathe a few times completely

in and out, sighing, yawning, causing tension to flow out of your system, and at the same time directing your attention inward.

- Take one crystal, its point directed toward your wrist, in your left hand. In your right hand, hold the other crystal with its point directed toward your fingers. So one crystal is directed inside, the other one directed outside.

This creates a natural polarity in your body's energy flow, causing the brain hemispheres to become more balanced.

With the crystals in your hands, lie or sit still during the playing time of the track. You will notice a clear flow of energy throughout your body. It will change in speed and intensity while the energy circulates. This can manifest as a prickling or tingling, a warm or a cold current. Just let it all happen, and after a while a pleasant equilibrium will follow.

This method works very well. The synergy between the natural shape of the crystal and the sound of the crystal singing bowls is strong and intense. After this meditation you will have a new reservoir of clean energy. This makes it less recommended for the evening hours. Start your day with this—that is the best moment. And do remember to flush your two rock crystals afterwards under running water, put them in direct sunlight for several hours, if possible, and store them neatly in a cloth until the next meditation session. •

READING LIST

Jonathan Goldman, *Healing Sounds: The Power of Harmonics* (Element Books, ISBN 1-85230-314-X)

Anneke Huyser, *Klankschalen en Hun Therapeutische Toepassingen* (Binkey Kok Publications, 1999, ISBN 90-74597-37-8).

Tosca Tetteroo, *Edelsteentherapie Van A Tot Z* (ISBN 90-325-0589-0).

———. *Geluk Is Een Edelsteen: Hoe Edelstenen Kunnen Helpen Gelukkig En Gezond Te Leven* (ISBN 90-325-0568-8).

Melly Uyldert, *Verborgen Krachten Der Edelstenen* (De Driehoek, ISBN 90-6030-292-3).

Renee Brodie, *The Healing Sounds Of Crystal Bowls* (ISBN 0-968079-00-8)

SUGGESTED LISTENING

Crystal Sounds (Deva) by Rainer Tillmann (Binkey Kok Publications, ISBN 1-57863-070-3). Meditations with the pure and harmonic vibrations of crystal singing bowls.

Sounds for Healing/1 (Soma) by Rainer Tillman (Binkey Kok Publications, ISBN 1-57863-072-X). Crystal and Tibetan singing bowls for meditation and healing.

Chakra Delight (Binkey Kok Publications. ISBN 90-74597-49-1) Book and CD by Dick de Ruiter and Rainer Tillmann. Pure chakra sounds with a clear explanation of each chakra.

Harmonic Overtones: Magical Vibrations in Voice and Music Book and CD by Dick de Ruiter and Rainer Tillmann (Binkey Kok Publications, ISBN 90-74597-48-0).

Crystal Spirit: Yatri (Pilgrim Records, USA) www.crystalmusic.com (this is not a recording of single crystal singing bowls but of an *armonica*, an instrument made of thirty-five quartz crystal bowls.

(The following CD recordings of crystal singing bowls are all available through the most extensive Web site about crystal singing bowls in all shapes and sizes,

www.crystalbowls.com. Here you will find links to famous writers and musicians such as Steven Halpern, Tom Kenyon, and Jonathan Goldman, all of whom work with crystal bowls.)

The Healing Sounds of Crystal Bowls by Renee Brodie
Travelling the Sacred Sound Current by Deborah van Dyke
Crystal Voices by Deborah van Dyke, Valerie Farnsworth
Celestial Memories by Elivia Melodey
Journey to Wholeness by Elivia Melodey
Ancient Music—Distant Dreams by Tasha Mato
Inua by Tasha Mato
Crystal Bowls in Concert by Ruth Rosseau-Clothier
Rapture by Ruth Rosseau-Clothier
A Labirinth of Sound by Steve Story and Celia Bourez
Sound Massage by Brigitte Hamm
Deeper by Life in Balance

TOSCA TETTEROO

has been working as a crystal healer and gem therapist for over 25 years. In 1981 she founded De Krater Gem Center, where all kinds of gem therapies are practiced.

Tosca is author of the books: *Edelsteentherapie van A tot Z (Gemstone Therapy from A to Z)*, and *Geluk is een Edelsteen (Luck is a Gemstone)*.

Tosca lives and works in the Netherlands as well as France and gives courses and workshops. Readers may contact her at *Edelsteencentrum De Krater, Oosterwoldseweg 14, 8421PA Oldeberkoop. E-mail: info@dekrater.nl*

DICK DE RUITER

has been is a yoga teacher since 1969 and has specialized since 1980 in the harmonic effects of sound. He introduced new age music to the Netherlands with his import company *Sono Music of Silence* and offered lots of seminars about the effects and possibilities of sound and special music in daily life. He is also the author of the Binkey Kok Publications Book & CD series. Currently Dick lives and works in the South of France.

RAINER TILLMANN

is a talented singing bowls player from Germany with many years of experience. He discovered the singing bowls in the 1980s, when he was playing in a rock band. From then on he specialized as a meditation musician. He discovered the crystal singing bowls in the 1990s, when the method was refined to produce perfectly and finely-tune bowls. Since then he has been selectively using these special sound instruments in his concerts and recordings, alone or combined with the metal ones, of which he has a collection of over 100.

Other Book & CD's from Binkey Kok:

THE UNIQUE SINGING BOWL

ISBN 90-74597-46-7

CHAKRA DELIGHT

ISBN 90-74597-49-1

THE HEALING TONES OF DIDGERIDOO

ISBN 90-74597-48-3

HARMONIC OVERTONES

ISBN 90-74597-58-0

Binkey Kok Publications – Havelte/Holland
www.binkeykok.com
e-mail info@binkeykok.com